Jo Macsween is a haggis aficionado, food lover and blogger. She grew up doing her homework in the offices of her family's butcher's shop, inhaling the wonderful aroma of freshly steamed haggis. Eventually joining the business in 1992, she is the driving force behind the evolution of Macsween of Edinburgh into a national brand synonymous with haggis-making excellence. Jo continues to be a passionate and enthusiastic ambassador for haggis, introducing a new generation to the virtues of this much maligned dish.

The
Macsween Haggis
Bible

Jo Macsween

BIRLINN

First published in 2013 by
Birlinn Limited
West Newington House
10 Newington Road
Edinburgh
EH9 1QS

3

www.birlinn.co.uk

ISBN: 978 1 78027 105 7

British Library Cataloguing-in-Publication Data
A catalogue record for this book is available
from the British Library

Designed and typeset by Mark Blackadder

Printed and bound by Bell & Bain Ltd, Glasgow

Contents

Veggie Delights

Snacks and Snastrells

For Dad, my Great Chieftain

John Angus Macsween
1939–2006

Haggis myths and mystery

Scotland's national dish is a source of endless jokes and stories and yet provokes huge curiosity. Unloved by some and passionately consumed by others, haggis has a bit of a bad-boy image to contend with. It can lay claim to an ancient lineage, a ritualistic annual celebration and an eight-verse tribute penned by none other than our national poet, Robert Burns. Its place in Scottish culture is assured for ever. But how did we reach this contradictory place of aversion and passion?

First we need to dispel some myths and go back in time. The biggest myth of all, in a way, is that haggis belongs to Scotland alone. It is an ancient and global food, as old as the very act of hunting itself. Our ancestors had the wit to realise that the offal of a slain beast had poor keeping qualities and so it was consumed first. I like to think of haggis as the celebratory dish everyone shared after the big hunt. With a more global perspective in mind, 'haggis' has been made from a variety of meats, depending on what animal had been killed and what else you had to hand. On the North American plains, it could well have been buffalo; in

desert areas, camel mixed with grains to add texture. And what do we have in Scotland in plentiful supply? Sheep and a lot of rain that is perfect for growing oats. So while names of this humble food around the globe may differ, the basic concept of haggis is present in almost every food culture around the world.

There is much discussion about how haggis came to be so closely associated with Scotland. The answer lies in poetry and a prodigious Scottish writer called Robert Burns. When he penned his eight-verse 'Address to a Haggis', he had no idea that it would be repeated around the globe every January at haggis-fuelled suppers in his honour. It is by no means his greatest work, rather something he whipped up as a bit of light-hearted entertainment for his hosts while staying in Edinburgh. Burns' tongue was firmly in cheek when he wrote this work, so this is not a poem to be delivered with a straight face but rather a light-hearted ditty with some nationalistic enthusiasm for good measure. (Sadly, it is delivered with deep gravitas all too often.) Burns unwittingly elevated haggis from its humble origins to something iconic; and, without him, there would be no high feasting on haggis in January. So I like to think of Burns as the patron saint of haggis, with 25 January being his annual feast day, when people all around the world sit down to a hearty plate of haggis and raise a glass to the wonderfully talented man to whom, in many respects, I owe my living.

Returning to the haggis aversion theme, it seems to me that the sources of most haggis-related anxieties are centred on either misunderstandings of the basic ingredients or (which seems worse to me) a less than satisfactory encounter with a poor-quality haggis. Talking generically for a moment – as all butchers and haggis-makers will have their own take on this – haggis is made of animal offal, fat, onions, oatmeal, seasonings and spices. Despite the renaissance of 'nose-to-tail' eating, there is still considerable queasiness about offal, and this can be the biggest barrier to people trying haggis for the first time. Traditionally, in Scotland, it was the animal 'pluck' that was used – the lungs, heart and liver. (If you have ever been to an abattoir then you will have seen that they come out of the animal conjoined and can easily be 'plucked' in one go.) Offal is extremely lean, which is why some fat must be added, both to lubricate the mix and to give it flavour. Authentic Scottish haggis is most closely associated with lamb offal, and that is what we have traditionally used at Macsween. It has a sweetness that is quite distinct from other animal offal, and I think that helps widen the appeal of our haggis.

I will confess here and now that I was not raised on lashings of offal. It is somewhat ironic that my father, John, who really put haggis on the UK culinary map in the 1980s, did not like offal himself and he never brought it home for us to eat. So I grew up with a policy of managed offal avoidance. The big exception was that, like my father, I did love our haggis. So why would that be? It is partly because the offal in haggis is minced, so the smooth texture – a bit of an issue for me – is avoided and instead the result is more akin to conventional minced meat. Secondly, the presence of other ingredients, like the deeply savoury beef fat, onions, seasoning, spices and the additional coarseness of the oatmeal, changes the dynamic again, so that it's really not like eating offal at all. Overdoing the amount of liver in the mix can really overpower the flavour and aroma of the more delicate spices and herbs. Indeed, at Macsween, we have never included any liver in our recipe.

There is one important element I have not covered yet: the outer casing. Is it a sheep's stomach, an animal bladder or what? This is often the root of a lot of deep-seated nervousness and misunderstandings about haggis. So going back to our ancient hunting chaps for a minute, in the absence of our modern-day pots and pans, an animal stomach solved the basic problem of how to contain the mixture and provided a handy cooking vessel to keep every-thing together while it cooked. This is really how the first 'haggis' was created. It represented the best sort of husbandry, as every part of the animal was used, a philosophy chefs are encouraging us to return to today in our approach to meat consumption. Until fairly recently, most proper haggis-makers still used sheep's stomachs for larger haggis. This is rarely the case now, as firstly the decline of local abattoirs in the UK has resulted in the skill of cleaning and preparing them all but disappearing, and secondly we don't eat in big groups anymore, so a smaller casing is more practical. What is used now? Proper haggis are made like any good authentic sausage, and that means using animal intestine. This often provokes cries of disgust, and yet I doubt such prejudicial responses are made about salami casings, even though it is the same material being used. Sometimes people do eat the salami

casing unintentionally and yet no one seems bothered. Indeed, in Brazil there is a dish called 'Feijoada' that is wholesome stew made with beans and meat trimmings which often contains small pieces of intestine. I ate it in Brazil a few times and enjoyed it. (Just for the record, eating intestine is pretty similar to eating certain seafood like squid – chewy, but perfectly edible in a good stew.) The best casing for haggis is ox or beef intestine, as it is wide and long. Pig and sheep intestines are much narrower and are usually used for making sausages. Where confusion has set in over the years is that people assume that the stomach or intestine is consumed as part of the experience, when in fact it is merely the container. Many haggis sold today, especially in supermarkets, are made without the natural casing (a man-made plastic alternative is used instead). I don't think this affects the flavour in a negative way; however, it does affect the appearance. For the haggis connoisseur this is an unthinkable situation, especially when it comes to Burns Night and the ceremonial address to the haggis. Stabbing a plastic-cased haggis is not to be recommended. It is both an insult to Burns' wonderful address and it could cause injury to the performer, as the knife is likely to bounce back and smack them in the face. The natural casing, however, allows a more theatrical and satisfying sinking of the knife when prompted by the line 'and cut you up wi' ready slight!'

So, what makes a good haggis? At Macsween, it's all about simplicity. We start by buying the best ingredients from trusted suppliers, many of whom we have worked with for years. We use our family recipe, virtually unchanged in 60 years, and, just as we have always done, we still make our haggis in small batches. The taste of haggis should be intensely savoury, full of sweet lamb flavours, with a clear presence of oats. There should be an awareness of onions in the background, and the right balance of spice and seasoning, so that you feel a gentle tingling at the back of your mouth but are not gasping for water. The right texture and mouth-feel are critical too: a good haggis should have a loose, crumbly, open texture when hot, and should not claw the roof of your mouth.

My family business origins are humble and small, beginning three generations ago with my grandfather, who set up a small family butcher shop in Bruntsfield, on the south side of Edinburgh, in 1953, having learnt his trade in the magnificent emporium of William Orr's in George Street. My father, John, joined him a few years later, and father and

son worked alongside each other until Charlie's death in 1975. It was really my parents who truly understood the potential of the quality of our haggis, and a key milestone in the development of the Macsween story was bringing it to the heart of London in the 1980s, when the top stores Selfridges, Harrods and Fortnum's started to sell our haggis. And so it was that a loyal haggis following began in England. This trend continues to this day, and we sell more haggis across the border than we do in Scotland – the English have a real appetite for good haggis, it would seem!

A second milestone in our history was the controversial development of the vegetarian haggis. First created in 1984 for the opening of the Scottish Poetry Library in Edinburgh, my father was rather bemused by the intense curiosity it created both in the press and the subsequent stream of fan mail he received from vegetarians who had been craving a meat-free haggis, and wanted more. Within a year the vegetarian haggis had become part of the Macsween repertoire. It may have started out as a bit of fun, but now, with around one in four of the haggis we sell being vegetarian, the joke has turned out rather well.

My brother James and I now run the business and face new challenges in keeping abreast of modern consumer needs while remaining true to our core value: making a great product we utterly believe in. How do you take a 'slow food' that takes around 45–60 minutes to cook, and make it more convenient? One of the achievements we are most proud of is the development of the 'microwave in 60 seconds haggis': a single serving in a pack that has no casing. The same recipe is used, but modern packaging technology has enabled us to meet the needs of consumers who are increasingly time-pressed. I have to say it is the product I find myself turning to the most.

Haggis has come a long way in the last thirty years and is increasingly consumed beyond the narrow confines of Burns Night. It is an incredibly versatile ingredient and, as I hope the recipes in this book will testify, a great culinary friend around the year and at all times of day. From breakfast rolls to stunning canapés and supper dishes, haggis can even grace your summer barbecue. Being crumbly and savoury, haggis acts as a natural substitute when you would normally use minced lamb or beef. It makes a great stuffing with meat and vegetables, and freezes extremely well. And as for the classic coupling of haggis and whisky, I hope I can encourage you to seek out some new drinking companions for haggis along the way.

A few notes on the recipes

Where I refer to haggis, I of course mean Macsween haggis. The microwavable haggis is a very convenient product consisting of two slices of haggis in a pack specially designed to 'steam cook' in the microwave in 60 seconds. It is very handy for quick meals and snacks, and I have to say I use it a lot. If you are not able to get hold of it, don't worry. Instead chop up the more conventional 454g ball-shaped variety into convenient amounts and microwave that; you can freeze what you don't use for another time or keep it in the fridge for a couple of days and make another recipe.

I would say that all the recipes will work with either traditional or vegetarian haggis, so don't feel constrained to stick to what I suggest. The recipes I specifically mention under 'Veggie Delights' are partly chosen to draw attention to what a brilliant ingredient vegetarian haggis is. I also happen to think that the meat-free version works particularly well in those recipes.

Enter the Haggis

It may seem a bit patronising to explain how to cook a haggis, but of all the questions I am asked, this is still top of the list. So treat this more as guidance notes and you can watch my step-by-step guide on our YouTube channel too (http://www.youtube.com/user/MacsweenHaggis/featured).

Cooking a haggis really is simple, I promise! The main thing to keep in mind is that haggis is already cooked when you buy it and all you need to do is make sure you serve it piping hot when you cook it again at home. Always serve haggis on warm plates. This makes all the difference, especially if you have a crowd to feed.

There are a number of methods for cooking your haggis, depending on the time you have and the scale of the occasion. Haggis responds well to wet heat and a bit of tenderness, and the cause of most burst haggis is that the heat is too intense.

Oven method
907g traditional haggis. (This is enough for four to five generous helpings.)

Preheat the oven to 180°C/350°F/gas mark 4.

Prepare the haggis for cooking by removing the outer vacuum-pack bag and wrapping it in a double layer of tin foil. Place it in a casserole dish with a few centimetres of water to keep the atmosphere in the oven moist. Cook for 1 hour and 45 minutes until piping hot. A clear indication of the 'piping hot' status is that the skin around the haggis is taut, and unless you have asbestos fingers there is no way you could comfortably pick it up. If you want to be a bit more scientific about it, you could use a kitchen probe. Gently insert this through the middle of the 'ear' of the haggis so you don't rip the casing. The reading you need from the centre of the haggis should be no less than 75°C (165°F).

Steam cooking

If you have a steam oven, you are in clover: haggis loves steam. Wrap the haggis in foil and use the steam-only setting at 100°C (210°F) and cook for 1 hour and 45 minutes. You can also use a double-pan steamer on the hob if your haggis fits into it, and adapt the timings for the poaching method below.

Poaching method

You can also cook the haggis in a pan of simmering water. Again, wrap the haggis in a double layer of foil. Try to keep the water on a gentle simmer – you're aiming to poach the haggis, not boil it! For this size of haggis, gently simmer for 1 hour and 40 minutes. Do be very careful when lifting the haggis out of the hot water at the end of the cooking.

Microwave method

If you are pressed for time, a handy short-cut is to microwave the haggis. Just bear in mind that you will not be able to present it at the table in its skin. The time taken depends

A BIT OF TENDERNESS

of course on how much haggis you are cooking and the power rating of your microwave. A 454g haggis, which feeds two to three people, will take around five to six minutes, and a 907g portion, which feeds four to five, will take around eight minutes. Remove all the packaging and the casing. Cut the skinned haggis into chunks and place it in a microwavable dish. Try and avoid the temptation to blast it on a high setting. The time taken to use a slightly lower setting like medium will reward you with a more satisfying result and prevent the texture going a bit 'airy' and crispy.

Cooking vegetarian haggis
Cooking the meat-free version is exactly the same process as above, and because the casings are man-made and therefore more robust you are far less likely to have a burst haggis to contend with. However, I do still recommend wrapping in foil just in case.

Why do haggis burst?
Most Macsween haggis are made in natural casings. The key word is 'natural'. Before being used, the animal intestines are rigorously cleaned and excess fat is removed by extremely skilled people. (Having watched this process many times when visiting our suppliers, I am in awe of their speed and accuracy.) Unlike man-made materials, natural casings need gentle handling, and if you cook your haggis at too high a temperature and in too dry an environment it will dry out and burst. Using tin foil goes some way to insuring against this mishap, but using a moist, moderate heat is the trick to keeping your haggis intact.

Theme and variations
If you want to add a twist to the awesome threesome of haggis, neeps and tatties, then I suggest serving cooked

beetroot. This earthy vegetable is brilliant with haggis, and the intense purple colour brings to mind the heathered hills surrounding my home. For those that like a sauce, I would recommend a whisky cream sauce. Beer and onion or mushroom sauces work really well too.

The Holy Trinity of Haggis

Perfect neeps and tatties

A Scot and an Englishman walk into a shop to buy some turnips. The Scot picks up a large purple and pale orange-coloured globe, while his southern friend selects a much smaller white-and-green vegetable. And therein lies so much confusion that means even supermarkets don't know how to label these vegetables without incurring the rage of some of their consumers. When I talk about 'neeps', I mean the large purple and orange coloured ones, known in Scotland as turnips and in England as swede.

Whatever name you choose, neeps and tatties go brilliantly with haggis. The secret of success is to cook and drain them properly to avoid a watery puddle on your plate. And just in case you don't know, 'tatties' are potatoes! So now that we have all that sorted, here's how to cook them.

Serves 4

1kg turnips
1 large carrot
1kg Maris Piper potatoes (or another good mashing variety)
100–150ml milk, warmed in the microwave (the amount needed will vary according to how floury your potatoes are)
80g butter (you may need more if you like it really buttery!)
salt and pepper to taste

First, prepare the vegetables by peeling the potatoes and turnips. Dice the turnips and carrot into 1cm cubes and cut the potatoes in half, or into quarters if large. Place the prepared potatoes in a pan of cold, salted water. You will need a separate pan of cold, salted water for cooking the turnips and carrot.

Bring both pans of vegetables to the boil, then reduce the heat a bit and simmer for about 20–25 minutes until they are soft. Test the vegetables with a sharp knife before draining, especially the turnips, as they need to be nice and soft in order to mash properly. Once the vegetables are cooked, drain them separately and allow all the steam and moisture to evaporate. This will ensure creamy potatoes and turnips that are not watery. To the potatoes, add the butter, some of the hot milk, salt and pepper and mash well. How much of these ingredients to use is to a large degree a matter of personal taste, so add a little at a time until you have creamy, lump-free mashed potatoes. To mash the turnips, add some butter, salt and pepper to taste. Turnips are really tasty with butter and black pepper, so don't skimp on these. Give the turnips and carrot a good mash, but I recommend that you retain a bit more texture, so don't mash until creamy. This allows for a good contrast to the smoother, creamier texture of the potatoes in the finished result.

Keep the mashed vegetables warm while you fetch the hot haggis to serve alongside. Don't forget to heat the plates too!

If you have any mashed vegetables left over after the meal, they are lovely refried (mixed together) with haggis for breakfast the next day. Alternatively, try making potato scones.

Clapshot

This dish is closely associated with the wonderful Orkney Islands. In essence it is simply an equal mix of neeps and tatties combined into one dish, with a few variations like onion added in. If you have a crowd to feed, this does rather simplify things. I also find that those who claim to detest neeps often rather like clapshot.

Serves 3–4
500g floury potatoes, peeled and cubed
500g turnips, peeled and cubed
50g butter
1 small onion, chopped
2 tablespoons chopped fresh chives
salt and pepper to taste

Place the potatoes and turnips into a large pot and cover with cold, salted water. Put over high heat, bring to the boil and cook for approximately 20–25 minutes until soft. Meanwhile, heat half the butter in a small frying pan over a medium high heat and fry the onion until soft and translucent. Drain the potatoes and turnips when cooked and add the remaining butter and the onions. Mash until smooth and then stir in the chopped chives, salt and pepper.

Haggis timbale

If you are looking for a more elegant way to serve the haggis, neeps and tatties for a dinner party, then this is a handy solution that you can make in advance and then heat when your guests arrive.

Serves 6 starters

6 ramekin dishes (6.5cm base diameter), lightly greased
    with rapeseed oil
390g traditional haggis cut into 6 × 65g slices
500g turnips, peeled and diced
1 carrot, peeled and diced
500g potatoes, peeled and diced
40g butter
2 teaspoons grainy mustard
salt and pepper

Prepare the mashed neeps and potatoes as per 'perfect neeps and tatties' recipe on page 18. Once the potatoes are mashed, mix in the grainy mustard. Keep the cooked vegetables to one side while you prepare the timbales. Lightly grease the ramekins with a pastry brush. Place a slice of haggis in the bottom of each dish. If you haven't been able to buy the haggis pre-sliced, then you can use a standard 454g haggis, remove the outer casings and then slice. If the slice is a bit big, don't worry; just push the haggis into a neat layer so you get an attractive profile at the end. Then spread approximately one tablespoon of mashed turnip and carrot onto the haggis, leaving room for a further tablespoon of mashed potato on the top. If you want to make it look really fancy, you could pipe the potato onto the top. Dot a few shavings of butter on the top of the potato to give a golden brown crust.

Bake uncovered in the oven at 180°C (350°F/gas mark 4) for about 20 minutes until piping hot and browned on the top. Serve with a jug of whisky cream sauce.

Whisky cream sauce with Arran mustard

Whisky is often seen as the obligatory drink to consume with haggis. However, don't feel you have to have it, as lots of other drinks go just as well, if not better. The pouring of whisky over haggis is entirely up to you, but I would recommend you enjoy them separately. Better still, make this easy sauce!

Serves 4 to 6 (depending on whether you are serving
   a starter or a main course)
1 dessert spoon rapeseed oil
30g or 1 small shallot, finely chopped
30ml whisky (choose your favourite tipple)
150ml chicken stock
250ml whipping cream
2 teaspoons Arran grainy mustard
salt and freshly milled black pepper
finely chopped chives (optional)

Heat the rapeseed oil in a heavy-bottomed pan and gently sauté the shallots without colouring them. Add the whisky and flambé to burn off the alcohol. Add the chicken stock to the pan and reduce the liquid by half. Season to taste. Add the cream, bring to the boil and then reduce to a consistency that will stick to the back of a spoon. If you want the sauce to be really smooth, pass it through a fine sieve. Add the Arran mustard, bring to the boil and do a final check on the seasoning. Finely chopped chives added at the last moment will give a vibrant green fleck of colour.

Whisky, wine, beer and other friends

The combination of whisky and haggis is a bit like an old married couple; everyone assumes it is a match made in heaven and that they never argue or fall out. I almost feel unpatriotic in suggesting that maybe they should split up and that the haggis should have a fling or two with a pint of beer. I do like whisky but I have to say I have never quite found such a highly alcoholic drink to be a great soulmate for any food, never mind haggis. So I tend to keep them well apart, preferring instead to retire from the dining table to a comfy seat for a long fireside chat with whisky glass in hand. And as for the dubious habit of pouring neat whisky over haggis, I can only assume that has been a necessity for some when faced with extremely inferior haggis! So in the spirit of haggis being a versatile ingredient (if you'll pardon the pun), I think we should introduce it to some new friends from the bar.

Wine

Although red wines are usually the best choice, blockbuster wines from hot climates (such as Australian Shirazes) are not what I have in mind. You most certainly need a wine of character to partner haggis, but too much body and alcohol tends to push its delicate flavours into the background, which is not the desired result at all. I have often found that South African and Italian wines seem to have the right acidity and levels of tannin to work harmoniously with haggis. In fact, acidity is a very important word: the juicy sharpness of red wine can often bring out the best in the haggis. A particular red grape that comes to mind is Barbera, and as this variety complements both traditional and vegetarian haggis, I have dubbed it 'the haggis red'! While red wines will generally work better with haggis recipes, some white wines do work well too. The biggest white wine success for me is Gewürztraminer from Alsace – the spiciness of this type of wine really complements the unique flavours of haggis.

Beer

I think one could safely speculate that Robert Burns could have enjoyed an ale of some sort with haggis when he ate it, if nothing else because the water was not fit to drink in Edinburgh in the mid-eighteenth century. In my experience, it is higher alcohol beers that work best to match the spicy character of haggis rather than a light lager or blond type beer.

There are plenty of UK beers to choose from and amongst my favourites are 'Dark Island' and 'Skullsplitter' from Orkney, and more local to me, 'Border Gold'. Continental beers such as 'Duvel' and 'Chimay', as well as some fruit beers, are also a great match.

Non-alcoholic

If you wish to avoid alcohol, then try some crisp, acidic apple juice, made with Bramley apples if you can get hold of one of the more specialist brands like James White. More recently I have tried some new combinations of apple juice with rhubarb which I think is a rather good pairing too.

Breakfasts

Haggis Benedict

My brother James loves to treat himself to this at the weekend after one of his long cycle rides. It's great with black pudding too.

Serves 2

130g packet 'microwave in 60 seconds' haggis
1 muffin, split in half
2 eggs
white wine vinegar
jar of hollandaise sauce
handful of chives, finely chopped

Break the eggs into separate cups or ramekins and add a half teaspoon of white wine vinegar to each one. (This trick will help the eggs stay in one piece when you poach them.) Heat a pan of salted water until it reaches a slow simmer. Carefully slip the eggs into the salted water and poach for few minutes. Meanwhile, gently heat the hollandaise sauce in a non-stick pan and toast the sliced muffin. Heat the haggis in the microwave according to the instructions on the pack.

Place the toasted muffin halves on the plate, butter them and top with a haggis slice. Place the poached egg on top of the haggis, spoon over the hollandaise and sprinkle with the chives.

Breakfast roll with bacon

If you need a quick hot breakfast to set you up for the day, then look no further than this. If you need it in under two minutes, ditch the bacon and just have a haggis express roll!

Serves 2
2 x 130g packets 'microwave in 60 seconds' haggis
4 rashers bacon
2 breakfast rolls, buttered

Preheat the oven to 150°C/300°F/gas mark 2.

Split the rolls, butter each half, and place in the oven to warm. Grill or fry the bacon, and when it is almost ready, cook the haggis according to the instructions on the pack.

Remove the rolls from the oven and place the haggis and bacon on top. Add some of your favourite relish or even a fried egg.

Vegetarian breakfast

Serves 2
130g packet 'microwave in 60 seconds' vegetarian haggis
2 potato scones
1 plum vine tomato
2 flat mushrooms
50ml extra virgin rapeseed oil
sea salt and freshly milled black pepper, to taste

Preheat oven to 170°C/325°F/gas mark 3. Preheat the grill to a moderate heat.

Heat the oil in a frying pan and brown the mushrooms. Season to taste and keep warm in the oven. Cut the tomato in half, season and lightly fry to colour. Finally, cook the potato scones until golden brown, remove from the pan and keep warm in the oven with the mushrooms and tomato. Cook the vegetarian haggis in the microwave according to the instructions on the pack (if you like it crispy, you could pan-fry it instead).

Arrange the haggis, tomato, mushrooms and potato scones attractively on warmed plates and enjoy with a good cuppa.

Omelette

Serves 1

60g traditional haggis
2 large free-range eggs
salt and pepper
small knob of butter
small handful of freshly chopped chives

Heat the haggis before you start to cook the omelette.
This may well be leftover haggis or one slice from the
microwavable two-pack. This can be done quickly in the
microwave, alternatively heat gently in a non-stick pan
and keep warm.

Crack the eggs into a bowl, season with salt and
pepper and beat well with a fork until thoroughly mixed.
Add the fresh chives and mix well.

Heat a small non-stick frying pan (try to avoid a big
pan as it will make your omelette too thin and dry). Add
the knob of butter and swirl it around as it melts to coat
the pan surface. Once it is foaming, turn the heat up and
add your egg mixture, ensuring that it covers the whole
pan surface quickly. Draw the edges of the omelette
towards the centre to allow any liquid egg to fill the gaps.
Sprinkle the hot haggis over the surface. Once the egg
mix is almost set, fold the omelette in half and serve
straight away. I like to have a good dollop of spicy tomato
chutney on the side to give this omelette a refreshing zing.

Main Meals

Haggis lasagne

Back in the early 1980s my father decided to type out a collection of haggis recipes he had been compiling and gave them out to customers in the Bruntsfield butcher shop in exchange for a 10 pence donation to charity. He always believed that people appreciated things they paid for, and over the years, I am sure many charities were very grateful for his old-fashioned wisdom! This is a variation of one of the recipes on that sheet. I have to say that when my husband makes this for our friends, no one wants any pudding, just second helpings of this!

Serves 4–6

For the meat sauce
260g traditional haggis
450g beef mince
250g lasagne sheets
2 tins chopped tomatoes
1 small tin tomato purée
2 medium onions, finely chopped
2–3 cloves garlic, crushed and chopped
a generous glass of red wine
2 sticks celery, finely chopped
1 tablespoon olive oil
1 concentrated beef stock cube
fresh or dried oregano
salt and freshly ground black pepper

For the white sauce
50g butter
1 heaped tablespoon plain flour
750ml milk
3 tablespoons freshly grated Parmesan cheese
½ teaspoon ground nutmeg
some extra olive oil for drizzling

Topping
Parmesan cheese
freshly ground black pepper

Preheat the oven to 180°C/350°F/gas mark 4.

First, make your meat sauce. Heat the olive oil in a
saucepan – a large frying pan with a lid is ideal – add the

onions and garlic and gently soften for 5 minutes, stirring occasionally. Add the beef and cook until brown, stirring to remove any lumps that may form. Coarsely chop the haggis and add to the mince, stirring until combined. Then stir in the celery, tomatoes, tomato purée, red wine and oregano. Crumble in the stock cube and stir thoroughly. Reduce the heat, place the lid on the pan and simmer for 30 minutes. Season to taste.

Next, make the white sauce. Melt the butter in a non-stick saucepan and stir in the flour, stirring continuously to form a roux. Allow to cook for about a minute. Gradually add the milk a splash at a time, stirring or whisking thoroughly to remove any lumps. Continue adding milk until you have a smooth sauce about the consistency of single cream. Add the nutmeg, stir for another 4–5 minutes, then season to taste with salt and black pepper.

Spread a 5–10mm layer of meat in the bottom of the lasagne dish and cover it with lasagne, trying not to allow sheets to overlap. Spread a layer of white sauce onto the lasagne, then another layer of meat followed by more lasagne. Repeat until the dish is full or you have run out of sauce. The top layer of lasagne should be covered with a layer of white sauce sprinkled with the grated Parmesan and ground black pepper.

Bake, uncovered, for 45–55 minutes, or until the cheese is golden and the lasagne is soft.

Haggis bobotie

Bobotie is regarded as the national dish of South Africa. It is traditionally made with leftovers from the Sunday roast and can be enjoyed hot or cold. In this version, I have simply swapped the minced lamb for haggis. Don't be put off by the long and, at times, rather strange ingredient list, it all works out in the end and is a great dish for feeding a crowd.

Serves 4

25g butter
1 large onion, chopped
454g traditional haggis
2 cloves garlic, crushed
2cm fresh root ginger, peeled and grated
2 teaspoons garam masala
1 teaspoon ground cumin
1 teaspoon ground coriander
1 teaspoon medium curry powder
½ teaspoon turmeric
2 cloves
1 teaspoon dried mixed herbs
50g dried apricots, chopped
50g sultanas
50g flaked almonds
3 tablespoons mango chutney
4 tablespoons chopped parsley

For the topping
250ml whole milk
3 large eggs
4 bay leaves

Preheat the oven to 180°C/350°F/gas mark 4.

Cook the haggis according to the instructions on the pack. Melt the butter in a saucepan and gently fry the onion until soft. Put the hot haggis into a large mixing bowl and add the fried onion together with all the other ingredients except the milk, eggs and bay leaves. Mix well and put into four 300-ml ovenproof bowls or one large ovenproof dish. Bake the mixture for approximately 10 minutes and then remove from the oven to add the topping.

Beat the milk and eggs together lightly and pour over the haggis mixture. Push the bay leaves into the topping and bake for a further 20–25 minutes for small boboties, 30–40 minutes for a large one, or until the topping has set and is golden brown.

Serve with rice, tomato salad and mango chutney.

Pizza party

My young godson, Charlie, has become a pizza addict since I taught him how easy this is to make.

Serves 1–2
1 pizza base
2 tablespoons extra virgin olive oil
1 small onion or shallot, very finely chopped or grated
1–2 cloves garlic, peeled and finely sliced
400g tin good quality tomatoes
fresh basil leaves, torn
salt and pepper
120g mozzarella cheese, sliced or grated
225g traditional haggis, skinned and cubed
handful of parsley

Preheat the oven to the temperature stated on the pizza base pack. You can of course make your own dough if you have time, but the pre-made ones give you a head start on the job. If you do make your own, preheat the oven to 220°C/425°F/gas mark 7.

To make the tomato sauce, heat the oil and gently fry the onion or shallot until soft. Add the garlic and sauté for about a minute or two. Add the tomatoes and season with salt and pepper. Cook gently for about 15 minutes. Add the ripped basil leaves at the end. (I must confess that if I am in a rush then I cheat by using a jar of tomato passata and thickening it with tomato purée if needed). Spread the tomato sauce onto the pizza base, followed by the cubed haggis and cheese.

Bake in a hot oven according to the instructions on the pizza base pack. Finely chop the parsley and sprinkle over the pizza before serving.

Torta salgada

This is a popular savoury dish from Brazil that is typically made with chicken and vegetables and cooked in a light batter to make a soufflé-style pie. You can experiment with your filling mixture by adding more spices.

Serves 4

For the pie batter
3 eggs
185ml rapeseed oil
500ml milk
80g cornflour
1 cube lamb stock
1 teaspoon salt
240g self-raising flour
2 tablespoons baking powder

For the filling
454g traditional haggis
1 red onion, chopped
1 teaspoon medium curry powder
5 tablespoons chopped parsley
1 jar diced marinated red peppers, drained, or jalapeño peppers

For the topping
sesame seeds or grated cheese

Preheat the oven to 180°C/350°F/gas mark 4.

Cook the haggis according to the instructions on the

pack. Prepare the filling mixture first by mixing together the hot haggis, red onion, curry powder, chopped parsley and diced red peppers. Set aside.

Thoroughly mix the milk, eggs and oil together. To this, add in the rest of the dry ingredients and mix until a smooth batter consistency is achieved. Don't worry if it looks a bit runny – the cornflour will thicken it up when baking. Pour about half of the batter into a large greased ovenproof dish.

Evenly spoon the haggis mixture on top of this and cover with the remaining batter. Sprinkle with sesame seeds and/or grated cheese of your choice, and bake in the oven for about 40 minutes, or until golden brown.

Serve with rice and salad, or enjoy cold with a picnic.

Haggis armadillo

This is my culinary tribute to one of Glasgow's newer architectural landmarks, the Clyde Auditorium, rather than a recipe based on some adventurous meat-eating!

WELL,
I WOULD
HOPE NOT.

Serves 4

4 chicken breasts with skin left on
454g vegetarian haggis
170g black pudding
250g streaky bacon
freshly ground black pepper

Preheat the oven to 200°C/400°F/gas mark 6.

Carefully slice the chicken breasts lengthwise so that you can lay them flat like an open book – do not cut in half completely. Place some vegetarian haggis inside and then close the breast again.

Then gently ease your fingers into the gap between the meat and the skin and push some of the black pudding into the space. You may need to stroke and smooth the top of the chicken breast to get a neat shape again.

To hold the haggis and black pudding in place during the cooking, wrap the breast with rashers of bacon, slightly overlapping to give an 'armadillo' effect. Season the chicken breasts and put them into a roasting tin onto the middle shelf of the oven for about 25–30 minutes until the chicken is completely cooked.

Ravioli with sage butter

This is a rather special recipe for me as it formed part of my wedding feast. My brother did a fantastic Italianate rendition of the address 'To a Haggis' brandishing a breadstick instead of his usual *skean dhu*.

Serves 6

600g tipo '00' flour (this is superfine and worth seeking out so you achieve velvety pasta)
6 whole eggs (or 12 egg yolks if you like a richer pasta)
dash of olive oil
225g traditional haggis
4 tablespoons mashed potato, cooled a bit
2 teaspoons whisky (optional, but a smokier whisky works best), otherwise use water
2–3 fresh sage leaves, finely chopped or 1 teaspoon dried sage

Sage butter

80g butter, melted
3 sage leaves whole

First, make the pasta dough. Sieve the flour into a bowl or onto a clean work surface. Make a well in the flour and gently beat the eggs into the well, gradually drawing more flour into the mix. Keep mixing in the flour. The dough will get stiffer and stickier. Flour your hands and knead the dough, adding just a small dash of olive oil if the dough is too dry or a bit more flour if it is too sticky. Knead until the dough becomes more elastic and silky.

This can take over 10 minutes, so be patient. Once you have achieved a pliable, smooth dough, wrap it in cling film and allow it to rest in the fridge for about 30 minutes.

Meanwhile, crumble the haggis into a bowl, and add the mashed potato and mix lightly until they are well combined. Add the whisky or water and the sage. Divide into small balls rolled lightly in your palms and set to one side.

Roll your pasta as thin as you can, ideally in a pasta machine. Press a sheet of pasta onto a ravioli mould, add the haggis mix, and cover with another sheet of pasta. Press and separate the ravioli, and dust with a little flour. Try to make sure that the haggis filling is well spaced inside the ravioli pillow to avoid air pockets forming.

Once you have your ravioli ready, add them to boiling salted water. They need very little time (around 2–3 minutes). Serve right away.

To make the sage and lemon butter, simply melt the butter gently with the whole ripped sage leaves so that the herb flavour infuses the butter. Pour over the hot pasta. Serve on hot plates to stop the butter cooling too quickly.

Hot baked tattie

I really do think it's worth the wait to bake your tattie in
the oven and not to express-cook it in the microwave.
Your patience will be rewarded with a lovely crispy skin
and fluffy mass of potato inside. If you are cold and
feeling sorry for yourself, this will hug and heat you from
inside like nothing else.

Serves 1
1 large baking potato
130g packet 'microwave in 60 seconds' haggis
coarse sea salt

Optional extras
butter
baked beans
grated cheese
freshly ground black pepper

Hot oven: 200°C/400°F/gas mark 6.

Give your potato a good wash and while it is still
damp rub some sea salt on the outside. Prick the skin all
over and bake directly on the bars of your oven shelves.
If you want to hurry it up, you could stick a metal
skewer through the middle of it to help the heat
penetrate faster. Bake for at least an hour – 1¼ hours is
better. The time depends on the size of the potato of
course! An indication of the potato's readiness is that the

outer skin will give when you apply some pressure, and if you poke a skewer into the centre, you should feel no resistance. Towards the end of the cooking time, heat the haggis in the microwave.

Cut open the potato and mash in some butter and then the hot haggis.

For a deluxe version, add hot baked beans, grated cheese and freshly ground black pepper as the finishing touch.

Scottish toad in the hole

Serves 4
454g traditional haggis, skinned and divided into 8 pieces
115g plain flour, sieved
4 beaten eggs
150ml water
rapeseed oil
salt and pepper
fresh thyme leaves (optional)

Sieve the flour into a large mixing bowl. Gradually add the beaten eggs and milk and whisk till you have a smooth batter. Season with salt and pepper and add a few fresh thyme leaves. Set to one side to rest. Heat the oven to 230°C/450°F/gas mark 8. Pour enough rapeseed oil into a roasting tin to cover the surface and heat till the oil is really hot. The secret of a light, unsoggy toad in the hole depends on this step, so don't be too impatient and pour the batter in too soon! Once the oil is sizzling, arrange the haggis chunks in the tray, spacing them out, and quickly pour in the batter so that the oil doesn't lose too much heat. Cook for approximately 30 minutes until the batter is puffy and golden brown. Delicious served with onion gravy or baked beans.

Shepherd's pie

Serves 4

454g traditional haggis, skinned and diced
1 medium onion, peeled and finely diced
1 carrot, finely diced
500g potatoes for mash, peeled and diced (or you could make
    a clapshot mix, see page 21)
100ml milk, warmed in the microwave
40g butter
1 tablespoon grainy mustard
salt and pepper
2 tablespoons rapeseed oil
grated cheese (optional)

Get started with the mash topping first by cooking the
potatoes until tender, drain thoroughly and mash, adding
the grainy mustard at the end (see page 18 for 'perfect
neeps and tatties' tips). While your potatoes are cooking,
gently fry the diced onion and carrot in oil until they
soften. Then add the diced haggis and heat until the
haggis loosens and heats up. Mix well with the onion and
carrot. Put the haggis mix into a pie dish and then top
with the mustard mashed potato. Grate some cheese on
the top if you like, and then bake in the oven at 180°C
(350°F/gas mark 4) till bubbling hot. Serve with purple
sprouting broccoli or a crispy green salad.

Flip-flop haggis

There are no actual flip-flops involved in this recipe unless you want to wear a pair while you cook! The name is more a reference to the fact that my first pancake of the batch is always a bit of a flop! Once I have the trial one behind me, I soon get the knack again. This recipe makes about 12 pancakes when I do it, but it rather depends on the thickness you prefer and the size of your pan.

For the pancakes
110g plain flour
pinch of salt
2 large eggs
275ml milk

For the cheese sauce
50g butter
25g plain flour
425ml milk
75g grated cheese
salt and pepper
freshly grated nutmeg

The haggis filling
454g hot haggis
15 kale leaves, chopped and cooked (I like to use Cavolo Nero and use about 1 chopped leaf per pancake. If you prefer, you can use fresh spinach leaves instead)

First, make the pancake batter. Sift the flour and salt into a large bowl. Whisk the egg and milk together in another bowl then, slowly pouring the liquid into the dry ingredients, whisk together until the batter is smooth. Set aside.

Then make the cheese sauce. Melt the butter in a small pan, then whisk in the flour. Cook for one minute, then gradually add the milk, whisking continuously. Bring to the boil and reduce the heat to a simmer for one minute until the sauce is thick and smooth. Stir in half of the cheese and season with salt and black pepper and some freshly grated nutmeg.

Now butter the frying pan and heat it well, but not enough to burn the butter. Use a cup or a ladle to measure out a portion of the mixture into the pan, bearing in mind how many pancakes you're aiming for. Fry the mixture over a moderate heat for several minutes, resisting any impulse to poke at it, or attempt to turn it until the surface has dried and the edges come away from the pan. The second side will cook quickly (I tend to have two pans on the go at the same time to speed things up). Completed pancakes can be kept hot by wrapping them in a clean tea towel and stowing them in the oven on a low setting; or they can be reheated later if you prefer. Heat the haggis according to the pack instructions.

Steam the chopped kale until softened. Spoon the hot haggis and kale leaves down the middle of each pancake, pour over a bit of sauce and roll the pancake up. Place the completed pancakes in an oven-proof dish, pour the rest of the sauce over the top and bake in a moderate oven (170°C/325°F/gas mark 3) for about 20 minutes until the sauce is bubbling and turning brown on top. Serve with a crunchy salad.

Flaky haggis roll

Serves 4
300g puff pastry
454g traditional haggis
1 egg yolk

Roll out the puff pastry into a rectangle 2mm thick.
Remove the outer casing on the haggis and cut it into
quarters. You now need to roll and manipulate the cold
haggis into a long sausage length for the inside of your
pastry roll. Once you have done that, place the haggis
along the length of the puff pastry, brush the outer edge
with egg yolk and roll it up in the same way you would a
sausage roll. Brush the top with the egg yolk and using a
pair of scissors or a sharp knife, make incisions along the
top of the sausage roll.

Place on a baking sheet and bake in a hot oven
(200°C/400°F/gas mark 6) for 15 minutes or until piping
hot and golden brown. Remove from the oven and allow
to cool for about 10 minutes. Then slice and enjoy with
baked beans for supper or, for a more swanky occasion,
they can be sliced to make small canapé-sized pieces.

Mungo pie

Mungo is my mountaineering friend who has climbed peaks and cliffs all over the world. His favourite home-coming meal is Macsween haggis. As a birthday treat one year my husband made him this pie and used off-cuts of pastry trim to form 'Happy Birthday, Mungo' on the top. He declared it the best birthday 'cake' ever.

Serves 4 (or 2 very hungry mountaineers!)
600g skinless and boneless chicken fillets, diced
200g traditional haggis, skinned and diced
2 large shallots, peeled and finely diced
2 whole leeks, cut into thin roundels
2 tablespoons rapeseed oil
320g packet ready rolled puff pastry (If you want to make birthday letters buy the 500g block)
1 beaten egg
salt and pepper

White wine cream sauce
50g butter
2 rounded tablespoons plain flour
1 glass white wine
500ml single cream
a good handful of fresh tarragon leaves, coarsely chopped

First make the filling for the pie. Fry the chopped shallots until softened and translucent. Add the chopped leeks and fry until they soften too. Then add the chicken and gently fry until the flesh turns white, but don't let it get crispy on the outside. In a separate saucepan, make a roux for your white wine sauce by melting the butter and stirring in the flour. Cook the roux for about a minute and then add the white wine a little bit at a time, stirring continually to eliminate any lumps. Continue adding wine until the sauce reaches a creamy consistency, but don't make it too thick or the pie filling will end up gloopy. If in doubt, err on the runny side. Finally, stir in the single cream and tarragon, and season to taste.

To compile the pie, tip the chicken mix and dried haggis (no need to pre-heat it) into a lasagne-type dish, then pour over the white wine sauce. Roll out the pastry top and gently transfer to the top of the dish. Make allowance for the fact that the pastry will shrink back a bit. Brush the top with the beaten egg and bake in the oven at 180°C (350°F/gas mark 4) for about 40–45 minutes until it is bubbling hot. Serve with green vegetables and mashed potato.

Veggie Delights

Baked onion, vegetarian haggis and feta cheese

We have enjoyed a great relationship with the Vegetarian Society, and our vegan-friendly vegetarian haggis has been Veg Society approved for decades now. They run a brilliant cookery school headed up by Alex Connell, and this is one of his favourite ways of enjoying our vegetarian haggis.

Serves 4

300g vegetarian haggis
4 large onions
1 tablespoon olive oil
1 tablespoon balsamic vinegar
200g chopped fresh tomatoes
75g feta cheese

Preheat the oven to 200°C/400°F/gas mark 6.

Wash the onions and place them unpeeled in an oversized casserole dish. Drizzle with the oil and season with salt and pepper. Roast for 40 minutes or until they feel soft. After 20 minutes place the tomatoes around the onions.

Once cooked, using a sharp knife carefully split the onions into quarters and pour the balsamic vinegar over them. Crumble the haggis into the middle of each onion and top with cheese then return to the oven for 10 minutes until the cheese is bubbling and golden.

Stuffed courgettes with sauce vierge

Our vegan-friendly haggis is packed full of wholesome ingredients including fresh vegetables, oats, beans, lentils and seeds – a great low GI food. Like its meaty counterpart, our veggie haggis makes a great stuffing in many dishes, including roasted meats like chicken and game as well as vegetables.

Serves 4
8 medium-sized courgettes
454g vegetarian haggis
2 tablespoons olive oil
110g mozzarella cheese, cubed
salt and pepper to taste

For the sauce vierge
150ml olive oil
2 cloves garlic, thinly sliced
4 tomatoes, peeled, deseeded and finely diced
6 tablespoons white balsamic vinegar
10 small fresh basil leaves

Preheat grill to a medium heat.

Slice the ends off the courgettes, and using an apple corer remove the inside of the courgettes, making sure not to break through the skin. You should be left with hollow tubes of courgette. Using the end of a wooden spoon, start at one end of the courgette and stuff with small amounts of vegetarian haggis, alternating with the

cubes of mozzarella cheese, and push to the middle. Then
turn the courgette around and start at the other end.
Make sure you are quite firm and that the stuffing is in
tightly. Brush the courgettes with olive oil and season,
then place under the grill for 15–18 minutes, turning
regularly.

Meanwhile, very gently heat the olive oil for the
sauce in a small pan and add the thin slices of garlic;
allow the garlic to soften but not go brown. Remove the
garlic from the oil with a slotted spoon and add the
tomatoes, white balsamic vinegar and the basil leaves.
Remove from the heat and allow the ingredients to
infuse gently. Season to taste.

Arrange the courgettes on the plate or in a serving
dish and spoon the dressing over.

Warm salad

Serves 4
2 × 130g packets 'microwave in 60 seconds' vegetarian haggis
200g baby salad leaves
1 Granny Smith apple, peeled and cored
100g red onion, peeled and thinly sliced

For the mustard dressing
40g coarse grain mustard
180ml extra virgin cold-pressed rapeseed oil
30ml white wine vinegar
salt and freshly milled black peppercorns

To make the mustard dressing, whisk the mustard,
vinegar and seasoning together, blend in the oil, season
and put to one side.

Heat the haggis in the microwave. Arrange the salad
leaves on the plates and gently pour over the dressing.
Break up the haggis and place gently on top of the leaves;
garnish with the apple and red onion.

Haggis and raita pitta pockets

Sue Lawrence first introduced me to the idea of stuffing
haggis into pittas with tzatziki, giving it a bit of a Greek
twist. My version is inspired by our local Indian
restaurant which makes rather good raita. The chillies
are optional but do give it a nice kick.

Serves 4
454g vegetarian haggis
4 pitta breads, toasted until warm and puffy
2 teaspoons salt
freshly ground black pepper, to taste

For the raita
½ medium cucumber, grated or finely chopped
200ml natural yogurt
large handful of fresh mint, chopped
½–1 fresh green chilli, de-seeded and finely chopped (optional)

To make the raita, wrap the grated cucumber in a clean
tea towel and squeeze out any excess water. Mix all the
ingredients together in a bowl. Heat the haggis according
to the instructions on the pack. Split the warm pitta
breads, then fill with a couple of spoonfuls of haggis. Top
with a couple of spoonfuls of raita. Serve hot.

Caledonian pakora

Many years ago my father and I were doing a haggis tasting at an international food exhibition in London. An Indian chef was demonstrating how to make pakoras nearby, and this is the result of fusion food at its best.

Makes about 20 pakoras
454g vegetarian haggis

For the batter
250g gram flour
pinch of bicarbonate of soda
pinch of chilli powder
salt to taste

To make the batter, add water (approx. 300ml) to the dry ingredients until you have a smooth batter that is neither too thin nor too thick, so that it will coat the haggis effectively. Leave it to rest for 10 minutes. You may like to add some extra ingredients to the batter, such as half-crushed fresh ginger, crushed fresh garlic, cumin seeds, whole coriander seeds, turmeric powder, fresh coriander, garam masala, etc. Form the vegetarian haggis into small balls, coat in the batter and deep-fry in hot oil until golden and crispy. Drain on kitchen paper and serve. Delicious hot or cold. Lovely served with chutney, chilli dips or raita (yogurt, mint and cucumber).

Pakoras freeze well so these can be made in advance if you are having a party.

Stuffed Portobello mushrooms

Serves 4
225g vegetarian haggis
4 large flat mushrooms
50g pine nuts
100g cheddar cheese, grated

Preheat the grill to a medium/high heat. Heat the haggis according to the pack instructions and set aside.

Place the mushrooms gill side down on a baking tray and grill for 2 minutes until the outer skin starts to wrinkle. Once cooked, remove the mushrooms from the grill and turn so the gills are facing up. Mix the vegetarian haggis and the pine nuts together and equally distribute over the mushrooms. Sprinkle on an equal amount of the cheese onto each mushroom and place under the grill for a further 2 minutes or until hot and bubbling. Serve immediately.

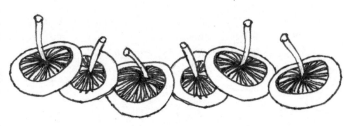

Spring rolls

Makes 8 rolls

225g vegetarian haggis
¼ red chilli very finely chopped
1 spring onion, finely chopped
1 tablespoon fresh coriander,
  chopped
2cm root ginger grated
40g grated carrot
60g bean sprouts roughly chopped
50g pak choi leaves, chopped

pinch of mixed spice
salt and pepper to taste
1 tablespoon soya sauce
270g ready-to-roll packet filo
  pastry (or even better, ready-
  made spring roll wrappers
  from an Asian supermarket)
2 tablespoons butter, melted
egg yolk

Break up the cold haggis into a bowl and add the rest of the filling ingredients and mix well. Then unwrap the filo pasty, taking care to keep the layers covered to stop them drying out while you make your spring rolls. Fold a sheet in half lengthways and brush the pastry with a little melted butter. Place a tablespoon of filling at the bottom edge and roll it up, applying a little butter to the top edge so it seals. Place on a baking sheet and brush the outside lightly with egg yolk or melted butter.

Bake at 180°C (350°F/gas mark 4) for about 8–10 minutes until lightly brown.

Serve with chilli sauce or hot tomato chutney and green salad.

Aubergine towers
with tomato concasse

This recipe is the happy outcome of getting to know Val Brunton, who runs a lovely restaurant in the Scottish Borders called The Sunflower. One day I called her up and asked if she would like to devise and cook haggis recipes with me live on stage at a large food show. Without a moment's hesitation, Val agreed and we hadn't even met. This is one of her very fine creations.

Serves 4
2 large aubergines, sliced
2 × 225g vegetarian haggis, sliced
2 × 125g mozzarella balls, sliced
olive oil for coating
salt

Tomato concasse
6 tomatoes
2 cloves garlic, crushed
1 tablespoon olive oil
sprinkle of caster sugar
150ml extra virgin olive oil
basil for garnishing

Slice the aubergines, place in a colander, salt and set aside.
For the tomato concasse, slice and dice the tomatoes.
Heat the oil and sauté the tomatoes and garlic, remove

from the heat and add the sugar, then pour in the oil and mix well.

Pat dry the aubergines to remove the water after salting. Heat more oil on a large baking tray, add the salted aubergines and bake for 10 minutes. Take another tray and place the 8 largest slices of aubergine on it, then place a slice of haggis on top of the aubergines then a slice of mozzarella and repeat the process another two times. Put in the oven for 15–20 minutes until golden brown and the mozzarella has melted. Place on a warm plate and drizzle the tomato concasse around the plate as a finishing touch.

Garnish with basil and mop up the juices with crusty bread.

Indian spiced pasty

Makes 6 pasties

260g vegetarian haggis
80g washed baby spinach leaves
40g butter
20g shallots, finely diced
80g button mushrooms, finely diced
½ small red chilli, finely diced
½ teaspoon black mustard seeds
½ teaspoon turmeric
½ teaspoon ground ginger
½ teaspoon ground coriander
15g desiccated coconut
salt and pepper
320g packet shortcrust pastry, ready-rolled
1 beaten egg yolk
2 tablespoons cumin seeds

Place the baby spinach leaves in a colander and blanch them by pouring hot water over them. Leave them to drain thoroughly before chopping. Leave to one side. Meanwhile, gently sauté the finely diced shallots in the butter until they go translucent but don't let them go brown. Then add the mushrooms and cook until they are soft. Add the chilli, all the spices and the coconut and mix. In a mixing bowl, break up the cold vegetarian haggis and add the shallot and mushroom mixture. Then add the chopped spinach, mix well and check the seasoning. Keep this to one side while you prepare the pastry. Using a saucer (approximately 15cm in diameter), cut out the pasty circles. By re-rolling the pastry, you should be able to get 6 pastry discs. Put a heaped table-spoon of the haggis mixture (around 70g) in an oval shape in the centre. Brush the outer edges with egg yolk and fold the pastry up to the top to make a Cornish pasty shape. Pinch the edges together and place on a baking sheet. Brush with egg yolk to ensure a golden brown finish. Sprinkle a few cumin seeds on the outside.

Bake at 180°C (350°F/gas mark 4) for about 20–25 minutes until golden.

Serve with beetroot relish. Delicious cold on a picnic too.

Veggie crumb cake with crème fraîche

This is another Val Brunton special.

Serves 4
454g vegetarian haggis
600g potatoes
50g butternut squash

For the coating
1 egg, beaten
2 tablespoons milk
breadcrumbs made with 100g bread and a handful of parsley,
    blended
4 tablespoons flour, lightly seasoned
vegetable oil for frying

For the crème fraîche topping
300ml tub crème fraîche
½ tablespoon wholegrain mustard
¼ tablespoon Dijon mustard
1 tablespoon whisky

_____

Steam the potatoes and butternut squash for 20 minutes.
Make the breadcrumbs. Crumble the haggis into a bowl.
Mash the potatoes and butternut squash (separately) and
allow to cool. Arrange three separate plates for coating
the cakes – one each for the seasoned flour, beaten egg
and the breadcrumbs. Fold the haggis and potatoes
together. Divide the mixture into eight even balls. Make
a hole in the middle, spoon in some butternut squash and
seal over with the potato and haggis mixture. Coat the
cakes with seasoned flour, then the egg wash and then
the breadcrumbs. Heat the oil and fry haggis cakes until
golden brown. Mix all the topping ingredients together
and spoon a dollop on top of the cakes when ready to
serve. Enjoy with a crunchy salad.

Stuffed red peppers

Serves 2
225g vegetarian haggis
2 red peppers
2 handfuls grated cheddar, crumbled feta or halloumi
jar of pesto (optional)
extra virgin olive oil (optional)

Heat the haggis according to the pack instructions and
set aside. Preheat the grill to medium/high heat.

Cut the red peppers in half, lengthways. Keep the
stalks attached to help the peppers keep their shape while
cooking, but scoop out the seeds. Place the peppers
under the grill with the outside facing up. Once the
peppers have softened a bit and the outsides are
beginning to char nicely, remove from the heat, turn the
peppers over and fill the insides with the vegetarian
haggis. Sprinkle the cheese on the top and place under
the grill again until hot and bubbling.

If you want to smarten the presentation a bit, you
could thin a bit of pesto with some extra virgin olive oil
and swirl it round the pepper on the plate.

Snacks and Snastrells*

*'Snastrell' is the term my lovely friends Eric and Clare give to food eaten in between meals or when they are overcome by an attack of the munchies.

Haggis toastie

This wonderful snack can be customised according to your taste, so mix and match your favourite condiments. Brown or tomato sauces are equally good.

Serves 1–2
130g packet 'microwave in 60 seconds' haggis
4 slices granary bread, spread with butter
Worcestershire sauce, to taste
wholegrain mustard, to taste
black pepper, to taste

Heat the haggis in the microwave and keep to one side. Spread the butter on the outside of the bread slices and place two with the butter side down on a sandwich toaster. Spread the mustard on the exposed side of the bread and then evenly add the haggis and flatten it out, taking care not to let it get too close to the edge. Liberally add the Worcestershire sauce and then add pepper.

Cover with the two remaining bread slices with the butter facing up, making sure they mirror the lower half. Carefully close the top of the toaster and cook for about 6–8 minutes. Remove from sandwich toaster and leave to stand for a couple of minutes.

Be careful when you take your first bite as the inside will be very hot!

Haggis panini

Serves 1
100g traditional haggis
1 ciabatta
4 vine tomatoes, halved
90g mozzarella
fresh basil

Cut the ciabatta in half, lengthways and toast, crust side
up on a medium grill for a few minutes. Spread the
haggis onto the untoasted sides, top with the tomatoes,
basil and sliced mozzarella then pop back under the grill
for a few more minutes until the cheese has melted.
Serve hot.

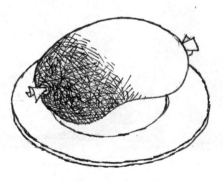

Haggis nachos

What do you get if you spend a weekend in Orkney with a friend who loves haggis and chillies and is completely obsessed with Texan swing music? This is the happy result of spending time with the polymath that is Duncan McLean.

Serves 1–2 (I could very easily trough these all on my ownsome!)
130g packet 'microwave in 60 seconds' traditional haggis
large bag of tortilla chips
tub of guacamole
jar of salsa
tub of sour cream
fresh coriander

Optional extras to consider:
jalapeño peppers, fresh chillies, grated cheddar

Heat the haggis in the microwave according to the instructions on the pack. Pour the tortilla chips onto a large plate. Dollop generous spoonfuls of guacamole and salsa over the chips and add a few jalapeño peppers if desired.

Once the haggis is piping hot, dot spoonfuls onto the top of the nachos, adding a few spoonfuls of sour cream and roughly chopped coriander to finish.

Eat immediately (with beer).

Haggis tostadas

Serves 1
2 flour tortillas
130g packet 'microwave in 60 seconds' traditional haggis
jar of salsa
tub of sour cream
fresh chillies, finely chopped
handful of fresh coriander, roughly chopped
handful of cheddar cheese, grated

Heat the microwavable haggis as per the pack instructions. You'll need one pack for each tortilla you make.

Using a non-stick frying pan (if it is properly non-stick, you shouldn't need any oil), heat the frying pan on a medium to high setting. You need the pan hot enough to melt the inside filling but not to burn the outside of the tortilla. Place one tortilla in the base of the pan and gently fork the hot haggis over the surface of the tortilla, along with a few dollops of salsa, sour cream, coriander, chopped chilli and a sprinkling of grated cheese. Put the other tortilla on top and allow the contents to melt. Keep an eye on that base tortilla and after a minute or so, very carefully flip it over with a large fish slice to toast the other side.

Once the other side is gently browned, slip it out of the pan and onto a plate. Eat immediately!

Bruschetta

If you asked me for my signature dish for introducing novices to the merits of haggis, this would be it. My friend Claire, already a haggis fan, loved this so much when she tried it that haggis has been the centrepiece of many of her party canapés ever since. I think tomatoes and haggis are a perfect match.

Makes 4 slices
225g traditional haggis or 2 × 130g packets 'microwave in 60 seconds' haggis
4 ciabatta slices, cut in half
80ml extra virgin cold-pressed olive oil
salt and freshly milled pepper
1 clove peeled garlic, cut in half
4 large plum tomatoes, cut into 1-cm pieces
60g red onions, peeled and chopped
15g flat-leaf parsley, chopped

Drizzle the ciabatta breads with half the oil, season and place on a baking sheet and bake in oven at 200°C (400°F/gas mark 6) for 6 minutes. Meanwhile, mix the tomatoes with the red onions, seasoning and chopped parsley. Microwave the haggis according to the pack instructions. Remove the ciabatta from the oven, rub the garlic over the surface to infuse the flavour onto the bread. Top with the tomatoes, red onions and parsley salsa, season, then add the spoonfuls of haggis and serve.

Haggis tacos

Serves 2
454g traditional haggis
6–8 taco shells
jar of salsa
tub of sour cream
flakes of Parmesan or cheddar cheese
lettuce leaves

Heat the haggis in the microwave as per the guidelines on the pack. Line the taco shells with lettuce on one side and salsa on the other. Fill the shell with haggis and top with a spoonful of sour cream and flakes of cheese. Eat immediately. You'll need a napkin as this is a messy eat!

Haggis tattie scones

This is a great way to use up left-over haggis and mashed potato.

Makes approximately 8 scones

200g mashed potato   50g plain flour
left-over haggis   salt and pepper

It is hard to tell you exactly how much flour to use as this will depend on how much mash you have. I would suggest that for every 200g of mash you have, you'll need about 50g of plain flour as an approximate ratio. As for the potato to haggis ratio, it is personal taste. A little haggis will give you a subtle fleck and the more you add, the more texture the final result will have. Mix the potato and haggis together and then add in enough flour so that you have a soft dough that will stand rolling out but is not too dry. I use my Kenwood mixer for this job.

If you overdo the flour, add a tiny bit of water till your mix softens again. Empty your dough onto a floured surface and roll out until it's about 3–4mm thick. Cut into triangular shapes by cutting round a small dinner plate and then quartering it.

Bake in oven at 180°C (350°F/gas mark 4) until golden brown – around 15 minutes.

You can also fry them in oil and cook on both sides till golden.

Haggis on toast

If you ask my young nephews, Charlie and George, how they like to eat haggis, this would be top of the list.

Makes 2 slices
130g packet 'microwave in 60 seconds' traditional haggis
2 slices bread, toasted and buttered
1 can baked beans, hot

This is so quick to make for kids' suppers and it is one of my 'lazy suppers' for consumption in front of the fire.

Heat the haggis in the microwave and spread onto buttered toast. I do think the 'buttered' bit is important here! The beans complete the feast.

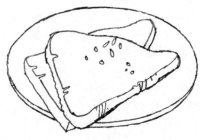

Sauté tatties, haggis, pancetta and apple

Sharp fruit flavours really complement haggis and this recipe brings together a few ingredients I really like.

Serves 2–3
250g small waxy potatoes
75g diced pancetta cubes or if easier, streaky bacon
1 large, crisp apple (try and select one that is quite acidic, like a Braeburn), cored and cubed
454g traditional haggis, cut into 2–3cm chunks
1 onion, chopped and finely diced
2 cloves of garlic, peeled and finely chopped
2 tablespoons rapeseed oil
1 tablespoon flat parsley, chopped
salt and pepper to taste

First, boil the potatoes (leave the skins on) until tender. Then drain and keep to one side. Meanwhile gently fry the diced haggis cubes in a tablespoon of oil for 4–5 minutes until they start to break up and crispen. Remove the haggis from the pan into a dish and cover to keep warm. Next, fry the onion in the oil to soften. Then add the chopped garlic. Add the pancetta cubes and fry for about 5 minutes. Add the cubed apple into the pan, season and cook for a few more minutes. Cut the cooked potatoes in half and tip them into the pan, turn up the heat and stir the mix. Fry until everything looks golden brown and slightly crispy at the edges. Remove from the heat, scatter the haggis cubes over the top and finally sprinkle the chopped parsley to finish.

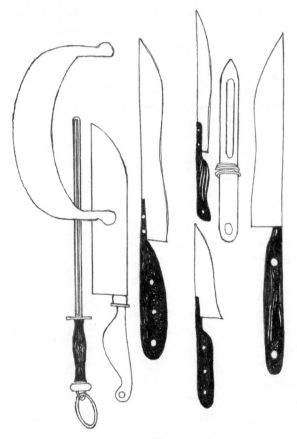

Party Treats

Baby Burns

These were served at our opening party when we moved to larger premises almost 20 years ago. They are a rather cute way of doing haggis and neeps in a bite-sized version.

Makes 30 canapés

30 baby new potatoes, waxy variety
454g traditional haggis, preheated
500g turnips, peeled and diced
1 large carrot, peeled and diced
80g butter (you may need more if you like it really buttery!)
salt and pepper to taste
parsley, to garnish

Preheat the oven to 180°C/350°F/gas mark 4.

Steam or boil the baby new potatoes with the skins left on. Meanwhile put the diced turnip and carrot in a pan of cold salted water and cook until tender – approximately 20–25 minutes. Once tender, thoroughly drain the turnip and carrot and place in a blender with the butter and season with salt and pepper. Purée the vegetables until really smooth and keep warm.

When the baby potatoes are ready, allow them to cool off and scoop out a hollow from the centre of the potato. Fill each potato with hot haggis and pipe the puréed turnips and carrot at the side to give a good colour contrast. Place on oven trays, brush very lightly with oil and cover with foil. Re-heat in a moderate oven. Serve with a sprinkling of freshly chopped parsley on top.

Haggis crostini

Makes around 10 slices
1 ciabatta
1 clove garlic, peeled
2 tablespoons olive oil
100g traditional haggis, pre-cooked
4 fresh vine tomatoes
basil or parsley
olives

Cook the haggis and keep it warm while you prepare the bases. Slice the ciabatta quite thinly and lightly toast. Rub a clove of garlic over the toasted surface and add a few drops of olive oil. Spread with some hot traditional haggis and add finely chopped fresh vine tomatoes. Finish with a sprinkling of freshly chopped herbs, such as basil or parsley, to decorate. I like olives, so I add them too.

Be warned, most guests eat so many that they have no room for anything else.

Wee beasties of the glen

Makes 15
225g traditional haggis
1 egg yolk, beaten
1 whole egg, beaten
6 tablespoons porridge oats, medium oatmeal (or panko
    breadcrumbs) for coating
vegetable oil for shallow frying
black pepper

Add the beaten egg yolk to the cold haggis in a bowl and
mix well. Add a few turns of black pepper to the mix.
Form into small bite-sized balls. Don't be tempted to
make them too big, otherwise the outside will burn
before the haggis inside is hot enough. Coat the balls in
beaten egg, then roll in the porridge oats or oatmeal (try
and opt for coarser rather than too fine an oatmeal for
this). Shallow-fry the balls in oil until golden brown and
serve right away.

These make a lovely starter, served with the whisky
cream sauce on page 24. Or stab with cocktail sticks for a
canapé.

SOS canapés

There are times when you need to rustle up a few bites to have with drinks and some canapés can either be a real faff to make or rather expensive to buy. Here are some quick ideas that are not too tricky to make.

Mini oatcake
Topped with chutney and hot haggis (for chutney try tomato, one with a sharp fruit like apple; rowanberry jelly is great too).

Mini haggis tartlets

You can buy these savoury cases pre-made. Fill with hot haggis and top with a chutney or red onion marmalade. The trick here is to fill them as last minute as possible to avoid soggy pastry.

Mini nachos

Pick out the biggest unbroken tortilla chips and put a dod of hot haggis and salsa on top, then sprinkle with finely chopped herbs.

Flaky haggis roll

Make the recipe on page 56 and slice into delicate rounds.

Haggis crostini

Make them using narrower diameter bread such as a baguette flute so that the finished result will be small enough to be eaten in one bite.

Mini haggis ramekins

Simply serve a very small portion of haggis in a ramekin, with a little bit of chutney or whisky cream sauce. Serve with oatcakes.

BBQ haggis

Our customers are a wonderful source of inspiration to us, and this recipe is the result of a conversation my father had when we were exhibiting at the Royal Highland Show. Determined to enjoy the rare evening of sun with some outdoor entertainment, a lady asked if it was possible to barbecue haggis. Not knowing the answer, he handed her a pack of our tiny canapé haggis and urged her to report back her results. True to her word, she did return next day. In this recipe, I have added a few other ingredients.

Serves 2 or a few more if served as part of a mixed barbecue grill
1 packet canapé haggis
2 tablespoons olive oil
2 tablespoons balsamic vinegar
salt and pepper
6 mushrooms, roughly chopped into large chunks
2 peppers, roughly chopped into large chunks
1 onion, roughly chopped into large chunks

Given that the haggis is pre-cooked, these are very quick and make a pleasing addition to your barbecue spread. The haggis will take less time to heat than the vegetables, so to avoid crunchy vegetables, marinade them ahead of time to soften them up.

Mix the oil and vinegar and add the chopped vegetables. Season with salt and pepper, then cover and put aside for at least 30 minutes, longer if you have time. Thread canapé haggis onto a skewer (with their skins still on), interspersed with some mushrooms, onion and pepper chunks. Barbecue once the coals are smouldering. Try to keep the skewers away from the most intense heat of the barbecue and eat once they are piping hot throughout. This will take approximately 5–10 minutes depending on the intensity of your barbecue. Delicious served with a tomato and chilli dip. You can eat the skins of the haggis or peel them off, as you prefer. Serve with (or without) sunshine.

Haggis on oatcakes
with red onion marmalade

My mum taught me to make a lovely onion marmalade
for serving with black pudding which works well with
haggis too. You don't have to use oatcakes; instead you

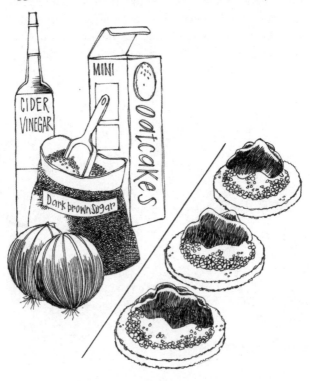

could substitute imaginatively with mini pastry cases, crackers or even thinly sliced toast, cut into squares.

Serves 6
454g traditional haggis
12 mini oatcakes, or use little pastry cases
finely chopped flat parsley leaves, to garnish

For red onion marmalade
3 medium red onions, peeled and finely chopped
2 tablespoons olive oil
2 tablespoons red wine or cider vinegar
4 tablespoons red wine or cider
1 level tablespoon dark brown sugar

For the marmalade, sauté the onions in the oil for 15–20 minutes until softened. Add the vinegar, wine and sugar and increase the heat. Once bubbling, lower to a simmer, cover and cook gently for 10 minutes, then cook uncovered for about 20 minutes, or until thick. Add seasoning to taste and set aside to cool.

To assemble, heat the haggis as per the guidelines on the pack. Slit open the haggis casing and spoon some haggis onto each oatcake. Top with a dollop of marmalade, sprinkle some parsley on the top and serve at once. Aim to fill and serve these as quickly as possible to avoid soggy canapés!

Filo haggis with bacon and pea purée

Makes approximately 8
340g packet filo pastry
225g vegetarian haggis
25g melted butter
2 egg whites, whisked
olive oil for greasing tray

Pea purée
100g bacon, dry fried
large handful of mint
500g frozen peas
knob of butter
300ml tub crème fraîche
100ml chicken stock

Lightly grease a baking tray. Bring the stock to the boil with the mint, bacon and peas and simmer for a few minutes. Remove from the heat. Put them in a blender, add the knob of butter and crème fraîche and season to taste. Leave to one side while you break up the haggis into 3-cm balls and set aside. Melt the remaining butter. Take a sheet of filo pastry and fold it twice lengthways to make it a third of the width. You will need one strip per haggis parcel. Brush the pastry with a little of the melted butter. Place one ball of haggis on the bottom of one of the prepared pastry strips. Fold a corner across the haggis diagonally and continue to fold, keeping a triangular shape all the way to the top of the sheet. Place your completed haggis parcels on your greased baking tray and brush with the egg whites. (Yes, I do mean egg whites, not yolks! I think this helps the filo pastry go crispy, and helps to seal everything in.) Bake for 20 minutes until golden brown. Remove from the oven. Put some of the pea purée on the plate and lay the parcels on top of the purée. Garnish with mint.

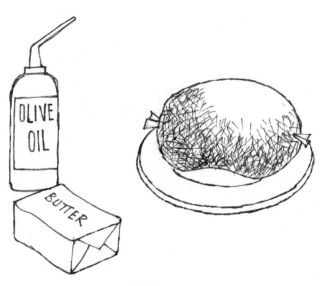

This wee book is only the start. If you want to learn more, you can watch Haggis TV as Macsween has a YouTube channel (http://www.youtube.com/user/MacsweenHaggis/featured), where you can see all sorts of things – recipes such as haggis nachos made in real time, as well as detailed explanations about preparing haggis, neeps and tatties. You can even learn how to address a haggis in style, tutored step by step by my brother, James.

If you are struggling to find a haggis near you, do get in touch via our website contact page (http://www.macsween.co.uk/contact-us) and we will do our best to help you locate your nearest retailers.

If you look up our Facebook page or our website, you can sign up to win a week's supply of haggis to help you try out some of the recipes featured in this book.

And lastly, I may have slipped up here and there on the recipes. If you encounter a wee mistake, or something isn't as clear as you'd like, I really hope you will tell me so I can get it right next time. And if you have any bright ideas for new recipes, then get in touch as I'd love to hear from you. Ideas that impress me are often rewarded with a gift of haggis.

Please email me at haggisbible@macsween.co.uk.

A few things you maybe didn't know about haggis . . .

1. One haggis, two haggis, three haggis . . . the plural term for haggis is haggis.
2. The earliest references to haggis (or a food that sounds just like it) date back to ancient Greece and appear in plays such as Aristophanes' *The Clouds*.
3. Traditional haggis is a great source of iron, fibre and carbohydrate.
4. Macsween haggis was a guest on the family game show *The Generation Game* in 1972. Contestants had to stuff haggis mix into a natural casing to an exact weight. It was a messy business.

5. If you live in the USA, Canada, New Zealand or Australia (and many other places outside Europe) then I'm afraid to say that haggis, along with many other meat products from Europe, is not permitted to be exported to you. Hopefully the regulations will change one day.

6. Type 'haggis' into Google, and you will have over 11 million results to explore. One or two will be about the Hollywood film director, Paul Haggis.

7. There is a Scottish sport called 'haggis hurling'. This involves standing on top of a whisky barrel and throwing the haggis (often frozen solid for added challenge) as far as possible without falling off the barrel or splitting the haggis. The world championship record currently stands at 55 metres.